THE STUDY OF
ECCLESIASTICAL HISTORY
TO-DAY

T0345981

THE STUDY OF
ECCLESIASTICAL HISTORY
TO-DAY

AN INAUGURAL ADDRESS

BY

JAMES POUNDER WHITNEY
DIXIE PROFESSOR OF ECCLESIASTICAL HISTORY IN THE
UNIVERSITY OF CAMBRIDGE

GIVEN AT EMMANUEL COLLEGE,
MONDAY, 26 MAY 1919

CAMBRIDGE
AT THE UNIVERSITY PRESS
1919

CAMBRIDGE UNIVERSITY PRESS
Cambridge, New York, Melbourne, Madrid, Cape Town,
Singapore, São Paulo, Delhi, Mexico City

Cambridge University Press
The Edinburgh Building, Cambridge CB2 8RU, UK

Published in the United States of America by Cambridge University Press, New York

www.cambridge.org
Information on this title: www.cambridge.org/9781107643628

First published 1919
Re-issued 2013

A catalogue record for this publication is available from the British Library

ISBN 978-1-107-64362-8 Paperback

ECCLESIASTICAL HISTORY

IT is a wholesome thing for a new Professor himself, however painful it is for others, to give an Inaugural Lecture. In it he can think aloud, as it were, over the duties of his new position, and the best ways of discharging them. It is good for anyone to ponder over a heritage into which he has come, with all its responsibilities and its inspirations. In this way he can form his ideal and see the work before him. He can embody that ideal in a confession of faith, by which others may know what to expect. For a moment he can depict his task as he would like to see it done, even when he foresees the certain imperfections of its accomplishment. Behind it all he feels deficiencies which he must always know better than others can, and the knowledge of these becomes a call to diligence, a commandment set by duty. So this afternoon I go on to do what is good for me even if it may be hard upon you. And if I am forced to speak more of myself than I hope I need ever do again, I ask your forgiveness and your patience. For I must speak of what I have learnt and of what I hope to do.

I need hardly remind you of what the Dixie foundation is. Sir Wolstan Dixie was a friend of Sir Walter Mildmay, the founder, in 1584, of Emmanuel College. Sir Walter meant his College to be a training-place to 'render as many as possible fit for the administration of the Divine Word and Sacraments: and that from this seed-ground the English Church might have those that she can summon to instruct the people and undertake the office of pastors, which is a thing necessary above all others.' And he said that the Fellows and Scholars were, above all, to devote themselves to 'sacred theology.'

He wished to strengthen the Puritan cause which, like others of Elizabeth's counsellors, he supported. And the piety, which, even in an age of great individual selfishness, led him to benefit at once religion and learning, is worthy of notice. His friend Sir Wolstan Dixie, however, in his benefaction, was more specially careful for the interests of his own family, which he wished specially to benefit. But the ancient trust has been, like the College itself, wisely treated and well enlarged, and the provision made for the Dixie Professorship was a token of its increasing usefulness. Emmanuel College, under the wise leadership of Dr Phear, first brought Dr Hort back to Cambridge, and then, upon lines laid down by that greatest scholar of a famous trio, devoted a large part of the Dixie trust to the needs of Ecclesiastical History in the University. It was a recognition on the side of the College, of the part which the Colleges of a great University should play in it. It is sometimes hard to re-concile the conflicting claims of the greater University and of its particular Colleges. I myself, for instance, have

7

worked in Universities where University and College were identical. I have worked in one where the Colleges were, as I thought, sacrificed to the University. Therefore I feel at liberty to state my own belief that in the happy, although difficult, combination of University and Colleges, we here have a priceless privilege. But the Colleges must contribute (the expression is not a purely financial one) to the greater body which shelters them. If they do so, the twofold tradition and the twofold life can work at their best. The College of Emmanuel, when it created the Dixie Chair, recognized that the Colleges should help the University in its care for higher studies. And it reaped a great reward. It has gained by the traditions which, under two Professors, have gathered around the Chair. The partnership of University and College has worked for the welfare of both, and incidentally for the happiness of the Dixie Professor himself.

Nobody here can speak the name of

Hort without the tribute such a life and such a work demand. He had laid his foundations in the study of the New Testament and of the Early Church. He was *the* great scholar of the New Testament Revisers. The Introduction to Westcott and Hort's New Testament is even more than an Introduction to one special field of Criticism, where Science is, perhaps, most nearly perfect: with the necessary change of technical terms from those of Textual Criticism to those of the criticism of historic evidence, it would become an excellent Introduction to Historical Study.

But this is not all. He laid the foundation of his Theology upon a wise and fearless study of History. The reward of those who love the past and face the present is to mould the future. That, I think, was what Hort truly did. His *Life and Letters* has been praised by a great French critic, Henri Brémond, as an illuminating work. It reveals to us a really great and profound observer, whose view of every

9

age, his own and others, was strengthened and enlarged by learning. As we read his letters we are forced to note the gulf which parts him off from the ill-balanced speculation of some German critics or the easy flippancy which is often taken for thought to-day. We remember that if his control and erudition recall to us Englishmen of long ago he was none the less trained and taught by the Cambridge of his day and taught even by the Natural Science which he, like Professor Gwatkin, loved so well. We take him, therefore, as a type of what Cambridge, at its best, and with its best, can do. For him, as for his friend Lightfoot, who rivalled his diligence and shared his spirit, History was the background of Theology. We surely cannot go wrong if in the foundation of the Dixie Professorship we see Hort's view of what History and Theology could be and do when linked together.

Mandell Creighton was the first to take and to enlarge the heritage. He

came to us here when he had been already
formed by the Oxford School of History
to which (as even its members confess)
we owe so much. Formed by its studies,
he had further been ripened by his teaching in it. He had all the habits and all
the gifts which a historian needs. He
was at home in the library and the study,
among his sources and his books: he was
equally at home in the world of his own
day and in the Italy of long ago. In
after years people wondered at the ease
with which he passed from teaching to
administration, at his equal mastery of
learning and of life. In his great book
on the Papacy during the Reformation
he taught us to see how one age moulded
its successor and he also taught us to see
men as they really were: he was never
shocked although he did sometimes shock.
Another even greater historian, Lord
Acton, whom we were also proud to
claim, criticized Creighton in his own
Review for a lack of moral judgment upon
individuals. I think this defect was caused

not only by his interest in the characteristics of an age rather than in those of its individuals, but still more by a tolerant humanity which had learnt much in the Common Room and the country parish as it was to do afterwards in the diocese. He had always carried his life into history as he was afterwards to carry his history into life. And it is hard to say whether he had gained more from learning or from life. We should remember that he had been trained not like Hort in Primitive Church History but in Modern History. He taught us what such learning would do for life, and upon learning he built his hopes. And in the more academic field we owe to his training both Mary Bateson, with her patient studies of medieval life and medieval municipalities, and Neville Figgis, with his brilliant study of medieval and later thought.

And the loss of Neville Figgis is so fresh in our minds that I cannot help but speak of him. He had guided us all, his seniors and his juniors alike, to a right understanding of medieval thought and we looked to him for even greater things. If, of late years, he had turned to other and wider fields, he had, none the less, with marvellous energy kept up his old historical work. Creighton and Acton and Maitland had taught him much, and from him in his turn we were glad to learn. As an admiring and sorrowing friend I should like to pay this tribute to his memory from a place which I would gladly have seen him fill.

A teacher is to be valued for those whom he has taught as well as for what he himself has done, and Creighton could stand either test with an ease which recalls his easy but brilliant speech. If Hort had taught us that the ecclesiastical historian must study his History and Theology together, and had trained himself in the earlier period, Creighton taught us to draw, as he had done, equal inspiration from a later period and from the methods of a more specialized historical school. He turned to the Great Councils of the fifteenth century and the Reformation period: he taught us to see how one age fashions that which follows. No historian can neglect either of these times or still more the many-sided process which joins the two together. So the field of work and the vision which belonged to the Chair were enlarged.

Then Henry Melvill Gwatkin succeeded Creighton. For me, who loved him as a friend, who had seen much of him in his later years, who had become his pupil disguised as a colleague in our labour together, it is difficult to speak of him as I should wish. In one special part of History, the age of St Athanasius and Constantine, he had done great work, and there we all were glad to sit at his feet and learn. One long-standing problem in particular he was the first to solve.

When Newman wrote his *Arians* Richard Hurrell Froude sent him some words of praise along with a significant criticism. He, like S. R. Maitland and Hugh James Rose, was a forerunner of our revived historic studies, and he reminds us strangely of some impulsive friends among our younger historians (if we are Radicals, there is no use in being nice, he said) : he had an unfailing eye for the significant ages of history and he read his authorities with immense diligence: he began with the Early Fathers, then went to Becket, to the Lollards, to the Reformation, to the Puritans (for whom he had a tender regard) and to the later Lutherans, always delighting in every age he came to, and quickly divining the questions which needed answers. Newman, Froude said, had not explained the Arian reaction after Nicaea. It was this out-standing difficulty which Gwatkin solved as through the mazes of that tangled age he passed with a Master's step. Like Hort, he had learnt most from the period of the Early Church, where every ecclesiastical historian should be at home.

There are two characteristics of his which I feel bound to notice here. Were I speaking in the College Chapel, which meant so much to him, there are others upon which I should like to dwell. But here I note these two.

The first is his wide reading among modern or secondary authorities. Before he came to Cambridge he had read, mastered and annotated that great work of Gibbon's which Prof. Bury, another teacher we are happy to claim, has enriched with his bibliographies and notes. This was Gwatkin's starting point and he understood how essential it is both for a historian to know not perhaps the impossible all, but all the possible best that has been written upon an age he is studying. Lord Acton had this knowledge to an almost incredible degree, and it made his judgments peculiarly weighty : it is something which a student must aim at if he does not wish to make unnecessary mistakes, to miss hints that would help him much, and to waste labour which others have worked to save him.

I do not wish to be misunderstood. There should always be close study of the original authorities and other sources. This Gwatkin knew both from his teachers and his own experience. We may recall that it is to him above anyone else we owe the rightful insistence in our History Tripos upon the use of original authorities. But he also understood this other essential, the use of great secondary writers, and this, unlike the use of original authorities, is something too often forgotten to-day. English and American scholarship seems likely to lose this special kind of learning, which marked the Caroline divines in Theology, and which equally marked older English historians. Prof. Bury, who has edited not only Gibbon, but also two works of Freeman's, can tell us how important this continuous learning is. But I find that to-day it is sometimes decried as needless, and this even by some who ought to know better. I am thankful therefore that, with much else, I was taught its importance long ago by my first teacher, who is happily my kindest and most learned teacher still, the present Master of Peterhouse. But I fear that if we lecture and examine our pupils as much and as often as we do, certainly if we lecture them more and examine them oftener, the cultivation of this historical knowledge will almost cease. I leave the topic to come back to it later. But I note that Gwatkin from the first set before himself this special kind of learning.

And another characteristic was the wide scope of his knowledge : there were really few periods of History in which he was not at home. He had, I think, some impatience of details : as he passed through the woods of History he liked to cut away the undergrowth. He aimed always and everywhere at forming for himself a clear picture of the outlines and the conditions of an age or a character. Hence he was a most successful teacher, the very phrases of whose lectures embedded themselves in the minds of his pupils. He had clear thought and clear expression, two faculties which are bound together, although some philosophers of to-day strive, by example if not by precept, to convince us of the contrary. Some of Gwatkin's writings (I will only instance the chapter on Tertullian in his *Early Church*, and that on Constantine in the *Cambridge Medieval History*) are hard to match and impossible to excel. With these poor words and this appreciation, true and sincere as he would have liked it to be, I pass from the memory of a friend I have lost to the study he loved so well.

I have spoken of the need for training younger historians in the knowledge of good secondary writers. I wish to speak of this at greater length because it seems to me most necessary for our own times. It is sometimes thought enough to say that History must be written from original authorities. But we should add the rider that it cannot be written solely

from them. There must also be a knowledge of secondary authorities. We cannot afford to neglect our predecessors,
and we learn even from their mistakes.
But that is a slight consideration com-
pared with others. Very often from a
secondary writer we get a clue or a
suggestion, which, as we think it over
along with our original authorities, illu-
minates a tangled period or a darkened
corner. If we neglect such reading we
often miss much, and certainly we have
often to do over again work which should
have been done once for all.

Not only in History but in Theology
also there are instances of a great loss to
learning from such neglect. Take, for
instance, in Theology, the best English
writers of the seventeenth century who
had this gift of scholarship. After their
day the politics of the Hanoverian Suc-
cession, with its isolation of the learned
Non-jurors, along with a change in the
trend of philosophy, led to a discontinuity
in theological thought and discussion.

Now, there should always be a freshness
of thought, a re-examination of conclusions already advanced, but too much
discontinuity in thought is a great disadvantage. The result of it in this case
was that English Theology became iso-
lated and distinctly poorer. In History,
and perhaps most of all in Ecclesiastical
History, something of the same kind
happened. If we turn even to inferior
writers of the age before, we often find
in them a knowledge of references and
of facts which gradually was lost as past
writers fell into disuse. Hence the nine-
teenth century started at a disadvantage:
it had to regain for itself, often under the
leadership of foreign and especially of
German writers, things which had been
matters of common knowledge. And although learning knows no iron law of
an eight-hours day, no age has after all
more than a fixed amount of labour at
its disposal.

And this leads us to another consideration. History is its own interpreter. Each

successive generation sees some aspect of the original evidence which it alone is able to understand. Of course, in doing this, it runs some risk of reading into the past something of its own mentality, something of its own modes of thought. But this risk is lessened if there is a continuous school of interpretation going steadily on from age to age and growing as it goes. There will, of necessity, be something in past discussions which each generation must discard, but there is much more from which it can learn. There is, however, a tendency to-day to think that we must start afresh with every generation, and as a result we often lose much. The interpretation of the eleventh century, for instance, suffered much certainly in England and even in Germany from a disregard of Giesebrecht's paper of 1866 on Papal legislation, and I could easily bring other illustrations. The modern process of education seems, however, both to lay too little stress upon this kind of learning and to leave too little time for it. The unbroken tradition of criticism and comment is, I think, a necessity of sound historic knowledge.

There must always be, to begin with, the careful collection and criticism of original evidence. It is in this process, even more than in discussions, that prepossessions have to be most carefully guarded against, and I would note specially that this applies to theological prepossessions, negative as well as positive. Then there should be a clear distinction made between the evidence and the conclusions from it, as well as a distinction between results that appear certain and those which are only tentative. In this respect our older English writers excelled, and here Lightfoot, for instance, was their true successor. Each generation knew exactly where it started and how it stood. But German writers of our day, and especially, I think, their ecclesiastical historians, have not this merit. Harnack, for instance, equal to Lightfoot in learning, compares badly with him in clearness of presentment, in sharp distinction between evidence used and assumed results. As we read we do not really know where we start or how we stand. There are welcome signs among us of a return to the older English style, and I might instance the discussions upon the organization of the early Church where Mr C. H. Turner has shewn us both how to examine and how to present the evidence we have. This is something every historical student should set before himself at the outset. In this way not only do we learn most surely for ourselves, but we also enable others in their turn to learn from us. This continuity of tradition is essential.

And now descending from the great men whom I have named I must turn to the duties of my new office as I see them, and to the hopes, indeed the fears, with which I enter upon it. Those who created it and those who have held it before me have given to it memories and have formed for it a tradition. As I have learnt so I hope to teach. I shall always be reminded that while Ecclesiastical History has the same laws and the same methods as every other branch of History, it can contribute much to Theology and the training which belongs to it. To find out the truth and to teach the truth: to spare no labour in the one, and to know no fear in the other: these are the very elements of the traditions into which I have come. But I do not learn that I am to have no convictions of my own, or that I have lost the right to express them in places, other than a professorial chair, where the expression of them is befitting. Yet there is one thing which I have learnt, even more, perhaps, at Cambridge than elsewhere: I have learnt that sound scholarship is a wonderful bridge-maker over streams of difference. I recall some discussions, for instance, of Reformation History where you cannot tell to what ecclesiastical camp the investigators belong. Scholarship has a brotherhood and a unity of its own, and in its pursuit one learns a tolerance which is a step to more.

But what is the special sphere within which a Professor of Ecclesiastical History has to learn and teach? Ecclesiastical History has no peculiar method of its own. Here, as elsewhere, the evidence has to be collected, weighed and tested, and the verdict given even if it must sometimes be an open one or tentative. And I hope that I shall never be ashamed to say that 'I do not know' or that 'I only know in part,' although that will not absolve me from the search after the truth. And yet I cannot profess that there is no difference between Ecclesiastical History and History of other kinds, and I do not think it enough to say that it differs merely in its field.

Ecclesiastical History is concerned with the history of the Church. And the definition of the Church belongs to history. The Church is a body of men made one by their common history. To use again a comparison I have made elsewhere, we may take the definition of a nation. A nation is a body of men made one by their common history: it differs from a State, it differs from a Nationality, the definition of which belongs to other Sciences as the definition of a nation belongs to history. It is history alone which can decide whether a body of men form or do not form a nation. The application of the definition has its difficulties and often gives rise to discussion. The same is the case with our definition of the Church: it has its difficulties and it causes its discussions. But we have learnt in other fields the advantages of the historical method applied to special studies. I might illustrate this from the historical study of Economics, where my old teacher Dr Cunningham led the way. Yet Economists have their difficulties and their controversies.

The application of the definition is fairly easy in the days of the Early Church, but in later days it has peculiar difficulties. We might satisfy ourselves with a very limited field of study although one that is fruitful and absorbing, if we took what I will venture to call the static test of unity. But a lesson which, although it has now risen into a philosophy of its own, some of us learnt first from Cambridge Theologians, is to look at things, at men and movements not in their static state of rest (although we do wrong to suppose that nature is ever at rest) but in their dynamic process of motion. Divisions have arisen, and have played such a great part in ecclesiastical history that they are painful to read. If we look at them as purely static the pain remains always with us and within us.

But let us look at our definition once again. Ecclesiastical History is the history of the Church, and the Church is a body of people made one by their common history, embracing their common characteristics, and their common tendencies. It is, however, to be looked at, not statically as if we imagined it to be fixed in any age, but dynamically as it moves through every age; one age with its process of life towards unity; another age with its diverse and manifold life moving, as it seems to us, when we look at it alone, towards disunion or even strife. But when we look, as we should always do, at the ages together and not at each age by itself, the appearance of division often turns out to be the sign of a richer and a fuller life attained it may be by suffering and loss. A growing life is always difficult to control and guide and men are apt to make mistakes. But in the end the larger union comes. It was so in the age after the Council of Nicaea: the Cappadocian Fathers and St Hilary of Poitiers followed St Athanasius: it was so in the seemingly hopeless disunion at the break-up of the Roman Empire in the West: it was so when the compelling hand of Charlemagne loosed its grasp upon the lands it held together. St Augustine of Hippo, St Gregory the Great, St Augustine of Canterbury,

Theodore of Tarsus, St Boniface and others at different times knit together again a Christian world which seemed to have fallen apart. East and West too seemed severed for ever after the Iconoclastic strife was over, when in 1054 Cardinal Humbert laid the haughty message of Rome upon the high Altar of St Sophia: again when at the end of the Middle Ages the Council of Florence failed in its task of unity: at every step restored unity seemed more hopeless. But to-day things are impelling East and West in a different direction, towards the unity which is part of the Church's heritage. And again at the end of the Middle Ages, with their real greatness which at last we are coming to understand, with their rich political thought, which Figgis among others taught us to appreciate, with their devotion which has become a proverb, in spite of all this the promised Great Councils failed in their work of unity and reform. These long ages seemed to end only in ripe

abuses and gigantic schism. Then came
the Reformation with its background of
great nations and their separate lives:
the crisis of thought and effort seemed
to have made disunion worse than ever.
Lutheran, Zwinglian, Calvinist, Anglican,
and Roman stood united only in dis-
cord, and beyond them lay their Eastern
brethren far apart. I need not carry the
story further. But once again the great
lesson of Church History is that no age,
no process, is final; to assume finality is
often to seek despair. To one age suc-
ceeds another which brings together the
forces which seemed divergent in the
first. And who that looks at the Christian world to-day with the wide and
patient gaze that history teaches can fail
to see signs of such a process, before our
very eyes and in our deepest heart. We
may, even if we do not fully understand,
be nearing the concord and the brotherhood which the early Christians knew.

If then we take our definition aright
we see that hopes of unity, the very pro-

cesses of unity itself, are not something which lie without our field, but are vitally its very own. If the ecclesiastical historian widens his knowledge day by day and age by age, if he keeps the courage, the tradition and the faith which are the spirit of his task, his study becomes for him an inspiration and a hope: it is to him, as Lightfoot said, the best of tonics, even in a day which seems anaemic. I recall the words of R. L. Stevenson, 'To travel hopefully is better than to arrive, and the true success is labour.'

If this be the special sphere of the ecclesiastical historian, it is well to look at some special needs of his study to-day. There are two such, it seems to me, which belong to material, and one which belongs to organization. We may take the former to begin with. It has been said that a wise man will never do for himself what he can get others to do for him. If this be the test of wisdom, then Britain has indeed been wise in its provision of original texts. We have been content to let other nations do this for us, both in the way of large collections, and in that of single works. We have our *Rolls Series* but we have little else; even that is far from complete, and the books in it are amazingly unequal. Some of them such as those edited by Stubbs from Oxford, and by Luard from Cambridge, are models of what should have been done in every case: Societies, moreover, which have undertaken the publication of Records do not meet with the support they deserve. And for collections of Documents, we have to go to past generations of Englishmen or to the great collections of France, Italy and Germany. Some of the work, which is really needed, could only be done by the fellowship of scholars throughout the land. A new edition of Wilkins, for instance, is urgently wanted, and many single texts await editors. There are competent scholars enough to do them, but some of these have to find support from other and more remunerative work. For in England to our shame, labour of this kind has to be its own reward. And upon that reward, with its glow of conscience and its praise from others, man cannot live.

There is, secondly, a lack of cheap texts for the training of students. Here we have now mainly to go to France and Germany, especially (if indeed we care to go) to the latter. Italy is organizing its school of History and bids fair to become second to France. For I think we may say that even before the war, France in its Historical School was ahead of Germany. But if we wish our own students to be trained properly there should be many more texts suitable for their use, and these England should provide for itself. As an illustration I can speak of experience gained in fixing special subjects for various examinations: at Cambridge, in London, and in Canada we were hampered by the lack of suitable texts, and in consequence some periods and subjects had to reappear with a frequency they did not deserve. Thus periods become hackneyed and hence our pupils start their career badly equipped. There are few modern English texts properly edited. This should be remedied. A young scholar could not begin his work better than by undertaking such a task: it is far better for him than beginning with an enlarged essay which will assuredly contain much that is immature and much that in later times he will gladly forget. To make a start in a field which he can cover, where the lines can be laid down firmly, and a foundation made for future work, is an excellent plan. I do not think we always choose our special subjects with sufficient regard to the future of our students, and in choosing them we are, as I have said, sadly hampered by the lack of texts. I wish therefore, that we had a larger choice, for as regards special subjects I remember, for instance, that because Figgis had to work at John of Salisbury as a subject for the Lightfoot Scholarship he was led towards medieval thought, the study which in his hands became so fruitful for himself and others. And I remember for my-self that a compulsory study of Erasmus for the like purpose, and of the eleventh century in another connexion, provided me with interests that have long been a delight. But owing to the lack of texts we cannot choose as freely as we could wish.

Theological students have not, I think, suffered so badly from this lack of texts as have historical students, although they are worse off on the historical than on the doctrinal side. The University Presses have always come to our help here and done some excellent work. And as a small beginning I may mention the help which we have been fortunate enough to gain from the Society for Promoting Christian Knowledge. Through the good offices of Dr Harmer, both of King's and Corpus Christi, and now Bishop of Rochester, the Lightfoot Trustees have kindly given the Society leave to reprint the texts of the Apostolic Fathers. We could thus begin even during the war when it was impossible to touch texts which needed

re-editing, and consequently we are provided with excellent texts for study in
class or privately, and that at astonishingly
low prices. And I may add that the
Master of the Rolls has given the same
Society leave to use a large number of
the Rolls Series in the same way ; so that
in the field of English Church History
and even of general English History,
there is a chance of similar work which
I commend to the notice of younger
scholars. But beyond this there are
many texts which sadly need re-editing,
and there are some which remain still
in manuscript. So I note as two great
needs for the study of History: first, a
revision of existing great collections or
even the formation of some anew, and
secondly the provision of cheap but ade-
quate single texts. And incidentally we
need badly more helps such as the admir-
able volume of Documents illustrating
the Continental Reformation which the
Oxford Press has published for Dr Kidd.
The same scholar is about to issue through

the same Press a volume of the same kind for Early Church History, and also a volume of documents (translated into English) for the same period now in the press for the Society for Promoting Christian Knowledge.

Then we may turn to organization of studies. Scattered workers need to be brought into closer touch with one another: thus they could not only gain the help of fellowship in their common work, but overlapping with its waste of labour would be prevented. Even inside our own University we might, as I suggest with diffidence, do more in this respect. In historical work it is essential not only to know what your own work is, but also to know what your neighbour is doing. I will not say that a historian should not mind his own business, but the chief reason for his existence is that he minds the business of other people: he has always to do it. Historical work in England, however, is extraordinarily decentralized and individual. Yet the success of the Manchester school shews what can be done. In keeping workers together, in keeping them abreast of what is being done by others, Historical periodicals are most useful. On the Continent they abound, but I am afraid our students do not fully understand what they might gain from the *English Historical Review* through the editing of which, although we must not forget the names of Creighton and Gardiner, Dr R. L. Poole has deepened his great claims upon our regard. I need not speak of other periodicals, either more general or more specialized, among which the *Journal of Theological Studies* holds a high place. And on special studies we can learn much from foreign reviews.

Such seem to me some present and pressing needs of our English work. We need to travel further and more rapidly upon lines already faintly marked. And I rejoice greatly that we are moving, as everything shews we should, towards the study of more modern times. On the side of Ecclesiastical History we halted too long at the barrier of 1800 or thereabouts. But now the date of the Fall of the Holy Roman Empire has been given up in the Regulations for the Lightfoot Scholarships in favour of the death of Pope Pius the Ninth, who, although with no special merits of his own, may have belonged to a more significant as he did certainly to a later date. And the Theological Tripos has also moved nearer to the days when we are making history for ourselves. Happily the Historical Tripos had never, I think, the same fear of more modern days. So I cease to be reminded of the ancient regulations which forced the infant Union Societies of our old Universities to discuss the merits of Queen Elizabeth or the execution of Charles the First with glances at the politics of their own day. We shall, I am sure, do well to study quite late Ecclesiastical History, although we can never forget the Early Church or the less tumultuous days of old. Personally I am not likely to lose my interest in Medieval times, or in the many dramas of the Reformation. But to-day calls, and rightly calls as I think, for a careful study of more recent periods.

For I am sure that once again our old Universities will take their rightful place in a truly national, even a truly imperial, plan of education, which will bring our ancient traditions and our older learning within the reach of a poor lad from a northern farm, of the son of an artizan in a manufacturing town, or of some wandering scholar from still further afield. We, even we in these modern times, may become medieval in our brotherhood of learning.

And I am sure that in the new days, which will be moulded by the old, many more will turn to the History which can give them so much. We shall do well therefore to consider carefully our plans, to build them on our hopes, not to restrain them by our fears.

And there is, I think, just now a special

call to Cambridge. History, especially at great moments in the national and imperial life, makes its appeal to all, and Ecclesiastical History furthermore is particularly essential to Theology, which has also its own wider appeal. But even more: Cambridge thought, and especially Cambridge Theology, holds a peculiar place. There is here an atmosphere which it is hard to describe but impossible to escape. Cambridge has rarely been in a hurry, except in the small detail of changing its examinations: it has rarely lost its self-control except upon questions of purely academic importance. It has never taken kindly to party strife although in its nourishment of individuality it has never tried to suppress strong convictions. It has thus become a storehouse of disciplined and powerful influences able to affect the outer world when it is calling eagerly for the help that we can give. Our past history has moulded us for future and wider needs.

No feature of our past University life

is more striking than the blending of
varied tendencies in College traditions
within the larger brotherhood of the
University. It is illustrated, if I may
speak of myself, as in a parable, by my
own experience. I pass from King's,
founded by the misunderstood King
Henry VI as a check upon Lollardy, to
Emmanuel, founded to foster Puritanism,
and, as I need not say, I do so with
hardly any sense of change. Yet, on the
other hand, King's was also the home of
the great Evangelical Charles Simeon,
where he dwelt during his magnificent
ministry at Holy Trinity : it was also
the home of George Williams, who
brought to Cambridge the influence of
the Oxford movement, and it was further
the home of Rowland Williams, who
wrote in *Essays and Reviews*. And now
from King's I pass to Sir Walter Mildmay's College of Emmanuel, founded to
support Puritanism, and yet it was the
College where Sancroft, afterwards the
Non-juring Archbishop of Canterbury,

was Master. It was also the home of William Law, the famous Non-juror whose writings so deeply influenced John Wesley, and at a later date John Keble, so that Methodism and Tractarianism own a common father in one commemorated in our chapel windows. I know of no more significant blending of diverse influences and varied thoughts. Such a history illustrates what Cambridge is and does; we can estimate the spiritual capital she has so long stored up by many a process such as this: now she can use it for a larger trust when it is needed for the enrichment of our nation. It is a magnificent spiritual tradition to have formed by centuries of internal fellowship and discipline and toil. Such are the processes of history which are the working of the hand of God. Such is the spirit of the Ecclesiastical History which we are called to teach, to ourselves and in our own day, to the world outside and for days to come.